The
MORTGAGING
of AMERICA

The
MORTGAGING
of AMERICA

BIBLICAL WISDOM FOR A TIME OF UNCERTAINTY AND CHANGE

D. JAMES KENNEDY, PH.D.

Edited by Karen L. Gushta, Ph.D.

CORAL
RIDGE
MINISTRIES

Fort Lauderdale, Florida

THE MORTGAGING OF AMERICA:
Biblical Wisdom for a Time of Uncertainty and Change
By D. James Kennedy, Ph.D.

© Coral Ridge Ministries 2009

ISBN 978-1-929626-03-8

Cover and Interior Design: Roark Creative, www.roarkcreative.com

Published by Coral Ridge Ministries.
Printed in the United States of America.

Coral Ridge Ministries
P.O. Box 1920
Fort Lauderdale, FL 33302
1-800-988-7884
letters@coralridge.org
www.coralridge.org

CONTENTS

INTRODUCTION

In 1994, Coral Ridge Ministries produced a TV special, *The Mortgaging of America*. Listening to the program today, without seeing the '90s hairdos and fashions, you would think that it had been produced this month, instead of fifteen years ago. In his opening remarks, Dr. Kennedy noted that the current president had won the election by focusing on the economy, "Yet, while the economy is on everyone's mind, Americans continue to enjoy one of the highest standards of living in the world. But will this legacy be passed on to our children?" He then noted that the national debt was over 4.5 trillion dollars, and projected to double over the next ten years. Indeed, that projection has come to pass, and America's gross national debt now stands at 10.6 trillion dollars, and today, as in 1994, "Americans are carrying more business and personal debt than ever in our history—mortgaging their future to 'live it up' today."

As Dr. Kennedy and his program guests pointed out, these matters should have been a wake-up call to our country to look at the fundamentals of our economy. Principles of sound economics were being violated—not only by failure to balance the federal budget, but by redistributing wealth through government programs and increasing government control of national resources by means of "environmental standards" and other federal regulations. As Christian financial expert Larry Burkett pointed out in the 1994 TV special, the problem was that the national debt and deficits were "running much faster than the economy." Some thought that the economy was headed toward deep recession, if not an out and out depression.

But something happened that was not anticipated at the time. By 1995 the stock market was on a steady upward track and moving into a period of tremendous growth, due to a new economic engine—technology stocks and the dot-coms. At the same time, the 1994 elections had brought an influx of fiscal conservatives into Congress. They worked with the president to reform welfare programs and balance the budget. The picture no longer looked so bleak by 1999. It appeared that we had dodged the bullet and we were saved from the economic disaster that seemed imminent in 1994.

Then in 2001 the unthinkable happened—America was attacked! For the first time since Pearl Harbor, we were attacked at home. The direct attack was aimed at the heart of our financial district—The Twin Towers, and our national defense system—The Pentagon. It was a clear statement—an effort to show us that these two pillars of our strength were not inviolate from attack by our enemies. Our economy lurched in response, but after a time, much to everyone's relief, it began to recover. For a time, those who had placed their hopes for economic security in the strength of America's economy and their stock market investments were reassured.

Nevertheless, the fundamentals of a sound economic system that Dr. Kennedy and others had addressed in *The Mortgaging of America* were still being ignored. More and more, people were looking to government, not God, to be America's economic savior. The principles of free enterprise, which harness and reward thrift, hard work, and initiative, were being ignored. More and more, government was taking a bigger and bigger share of its citizens' wealth—in effect stealing from one group in order to give to another more favored group. Our nation's gross national debt, which has increased by 42 percent since 1994, now makes our children and our grandchildren vulnerable to the whims of our overseas creditors—a number of whom are not necessarily our friends.

As we face this dismal picture, is there hope? Is there a way out of the current "crisis," which we are being told will take years to overcome? Yes—we believe there is. God is still sovereign and He will listen to His people, if they humbly approach Him in repentance (2 Corinthians 7:8-10), seek to cleanse their ways (James 4:8; I John 1:9), and act according to His divine laws (Nehemiah 9:13).

Therefore, Coral Ridge Ministries is presenting Dr. D. James Kennedy's words of biblical wisdom in this set of six sermons, preached over a period of more than twenty-five years. Each deals with key topics of biblical principles of economics. We trust that in these uncertain times, you will be encouraged and heartened as you read these chapters, and our prayer is that these fundamental biblical principles will help you in two ways. First, we trust that they will give you understanding that will aid you in making your own personal financial decisions. Second, we also hope that they will aid you in evaluating the policy proposals that are being put before our nation by our elected leaders—those who are now making the decisions that will impact our country for generations to come.

In chapter one, "The Bible and Economics," Dr. Kennedy sets forth key biblical principles concerning private property, work, justice, and charity. His application of these principles is as timely now as it was when this sermon was originally preached in 1983.

Chapter two, "The Christian View of Economics," affirms both the value of work and the responsibility we have to use our economic resources to demonstrate our honesty and our charity. In this chapter, preached 20 years after "The Bible and Economics," Dr. Kennedy returns to many of the same principles he set forth earlier. In this sermon, he elaborates on them in a way that provides additional understanding of their importance and their current application.

Chapter three answers the question, "Does the Bible Teach Socialism?" When the word *socialism* entered the political discourse during the recent election, it was essentially scoffed at by the mainstream media, and most pundits on both sides were quick to say that we should not use the word to describe any candidate's policy proposals. Yet over twenty-five years ago, Dr. Kennedy clearly identified the traits of socialism that were already evident in our society, and he showed why socialism is antithetical to biblical principles. He clearly warned of the disastrous consequences that will come to any nation that follows its path.

"Christianity and the Federal Deficit" addresses the problem of spiraling debt at its root causes. The biblical principles that Dr. Kennedy outlined in 1989 are just as relevant today as they were then. We would be foolish to think that our economy can get back on track if we do not give heed to them.

"Give Me, Give Me, Give Me!" is the most recent of the sermons included in this collection and addresses a prevalent attitude in today's society. When he preached it, Dr. Kennedy was addressing a congregation reeling from the impact of hurricane Wilma. Homes, neighborhoods, businesses, and even their own church building had been affected by the 125-mile-an hour winds that had torn through Fort Lauderdale. Roofing had been ripped off the church, and water had damaged the sanctuary. In what is one of his most poignant sermons, Dr. Kennedy challenged his congregation to avoid the mentality of a culture that is always looking for a handout.

The final chapter, "A Matter of Profit and Loss," will surely be an encouragement to every Christian. It puts our present economic woes in perspective—eternal perspective. "For what will it profit a man if he gains the whole world, and loses his own soul?" (Mark 8:36). Our *true enterprise* is not here on earth— laying up treasures, "where moth and rust destroy and where thieves break in and steal" (Matthew 6:19). Any enterprise we undertake as Christians should be done out of gratitude and for the glory of Him who gave Himself for us, paying the debt we could never pay. Engaging in such work lays up "treasures in heaven, where neither moth nor rust destroys and where thieves do not break in and steal" (Matthew 6:20).

Karen L. Gushta
Coral Ridge Ministries
Fort Lauderdale, Florida

CHAPTER ONE

THE BIBLE
AND ECONOMICS[*]

The first paragraph below could have been written yesterday. Once again the vision of America as a land of "unparalleled opportunity" is tarnishing. Some say we are facing "the worst economy since the Great Depression," and others, "the worst economy since Jimmy Carter." America must respond— but everyone is asking, "How?" What principles can guide us? Is there a sure path to follow?

In this chapter, Dr. Kennedy sets forth a number of biblical principles of economics. He discusses private property, work, justice, and charity. He also shows how our nation is, in the name of "social justice," edging closer and closer to becoming a welfare state and he outlines the consequences of this. Without a doubt, this chapter is as timely now as when it was originally preached.

* This was originally preached by Dr. D. James Kennedy at Coral Ridge Presbyterian Church in Fort Lauderdale, Florida, on May 22, 1983.

"For even when we were with you, we commanded
you this: If anyone will not work, neither shall he eat."
—II Thessalonians 3:10

America has always been a wonder nation in the eyes of the world: the home of the free and the land of the brave. It has been the land of unparalleled opportunity. It has been like a city set upon a hill, shining in the noonday sun and sending forth its gleams to the ends of the earth—to the desolate, the destitute, the tempest-tossed who came by the millions to these shores of plenty. Yet today, for many it seems the dream has faded. The opportunities, for a large number of Americans, seem to be gone. Many are dissatisfied. Something seems to have gone wrong. Most folks cannot quite put their finger on just what that is.

I would like to talk to you about a very significant part of the problem that faces our country today, a part that is not popular to talk about. I want to talk to you about what the Bible says about economics. Most of our politicians shy away from this subject like it was the plague. Few people ever hear what God has to say about economics. This may seem to some like a recondite subject and theoretical; but it is very practical. Each one of us lives life enmeshed in the world of economics. It is well that we understand it and perhaps see where this nation went wrong. Its economic deviance has happened, for most people, so slowly and so gradually. It has taken decades to transpire. Therefore, it is difficult to perceive. So let us step aside and, through the glass of God's Word, look at what is happening in America today to see how we went wrong.

GOD ON PRIVATE PROPERTY

The Bible is not a textbook on economics. It is not a textbook on politics or science either.

However, it has a great deal to say about those subjects. What it says is true and valuable. From those teachings we may erect certain systems and derive an understanding about those subjects. The Bible certainly has much to say about *private property*. It makes clear that man has an interest in the possession of his own property. This interest is guarded by the flaming sword of divine vengeance guaranteed in the Decalogue in the Eighth Commandment—"You shall not steal."

God knows that for us to fulfill our probation in this world, it will be necessary for us to make use of the things of this world. If we are going to demonstrate our faithfulness in little things, if we are going to demonstrate our honesty, if we are going to demonstrate our charity, we will need to exercise private ownership. Therefore, God has guaranteed it.

This alone rules out certain systems. It rules out systems that deny private property, such as *communism* or various aspects of *socialism* that would deprive man of his rights in property. The Bible has a good deal to say about other things that impinge upon economic matters, such as greed and covetousness and envy and jealousy. It also has something to say about work.

GOD HAS ORDAINED WORK

Many people suppose that work is a curse to be avoided, if at all possible, and an activity to be involved in only when necessary. This is not the case. God ordained work *before* the fall. It is not part of the curse. Adam was commanded to tend the garden before he fell into sin. Even after sin, though it is greatly aggravated by the results of the fall and the curse, it is still true that work occupies a very important position in man's life. Without work, it is impossible for any human being to fulfill the probation that God has given him in this life.

In today's text, Paul minces no words about loafers: "For even when we were with you, we commanded you this: If anyone will not work, neither shall he eat" (II Thessalonians 3:10). You would listen a long time before you heard those words today. The Apostle knew that man inclines toward evil, and so he inclines toward idleness and laziness. A man will avoid all opportunities to work if he can, but the Apostle makes it clear that if man will not work, he is not to eat.

This does not refer to a person who is not able to work. The

Scripture has a great deal to say about caring for the lame, the blind, the sick, the infirm, the aged, and the young; but if anyone *will not* work, then neither let him eat.

Because of the prevailing politics of guilt, most people will feel a twinge of guilt when they hear those words—as if they were words without compassion. May I say to you that this is the most compassionate statement on the subject of economics that has ever been made. Were that not to a large degree followed, there would be wholesale famine and starvation plaguing the world. So let it be underscored and proclaimed in bold and capital letters: "If anyone will not work, neither let him eat!"

JUSTICE DOES NOT DISCRIMINATE
The Bible says so much about *justice* and *charity*. I would like to address your attention to these today as they impinge upon this subject of the Scripture and economics. Here, I think, is the greatest source of confusion in our time! A confounding of justice and charity is bringing about our lack of productivity, slowing down the growth of the Gross National Product, throwing people out of work, and creating all sorts of economic chaos in the nation today. It is vitally important that people understand the difference between the two. Probably 95 percent of Americans could not clearly define either justice or charity.

Let us look at them for a moment. What is *justice?* The first thing to remember is that justice is blind. We have been trying to tell people that for many centuries. What leaps to our minds is the famous statue of Justice with scales held high, sword in hand, and blindfold over her eyes. Justice does not discriminate. It does not see whether one is of high or low class, rich or poor, black or white, working or not working. It does not see one's national origin. It does not detect one's religion. It treats all alike and all equally. That is the essence of justice. The statue would also remind us by the sword that it is enforced by the coercive power of the state. The principle business of the state, of law, and of government is the enforcement of justice, the protecting of the rights of all people *equally*. Justice does not discriminate.

CHARITY IS DISCRIMINATING AND VOLUNTARY

On the other hand, charity is not based in coercion—nor is it blind. Charity is *discriminating* and *voluntary*. If you remove the voluntary aspect of charity, it ceases to be charity. What would you think if, after Robin Hood had placed his sword at the throat of some rich man and deprived him of his purse and scattered his coins to the poor, that rich man told his friends how charitable he had been to the poor? There was no charity on the rich man's part in what happened—not a penny's worth! If you take away the voluntary aspect of charity, it becomes despoliation. It is legal plunder. It is robbery, not charity. Confusing justice and charity has produced something called "social justice," the basis for the welfare state. *Social justice* is having a tremendous negative impact upon the economic well-being of this country.

You cannot have charity or justice when you forcibly take money from A and give it to B. You don't have charity, because it was not freely willed. You don't have justice, because you are not treating A and B alike, but are taking from one and giving to the other. The rights of each have not been protected, but stripped.

SOCIAL JUSTICE AND THE REDISTRIBUTION OF WEALTH

Behind this notion of *social justice* lurks the idea that there must be a more equitable distribution of wealth. We hear this repeatedly. We have heard this so many times that I am sure the majority of Americans have accepted it—"There must be a more just distribution of wealth!" Behind that notion is the idea of a static economic pie of one size that remains the same size. Many think it is obvious that if you have eight people and one pie and you end up with a very large piece of this pie, you are despoiling somebody else. The only reason you have more is because somebody else has less; therefore we need to intervene with justice. Justice means we are going to take away a part of your pie and give it to somebody who has less. That concept has become so prevalent in America that it needs to be carefully examined.

First of all, this notion accepts the static view of economics typical of *communism* and totally alien to the free enterprise system that made this country prosperous. Free market economics postulates a growing economic pie and by no means indicates that if one person has more, another person must inevitably have less. It postulates exactly the opposite. If one person has more, in the process of getting more, he has succeeded in contributing to the enlargement of every other piece. For example, Henry Ford was born into this world a poor man. He left the world worth hundreds of millions of dollars. From the static point of view, the communist point of view, he had hundreds of millions of dollars by plundering everyone. He had despoiled all of us, taken part of our wealth. If justice will prevail, we shall take that away from him and divide it among ourselves, because he has impoverished us by his gain.

Is that true? Is not the very opposite true? Is not the truth that every one of us is richer because of Henry Ford—or would you have preferred to walk to church today or ridden a horse?

The only time we do not gain when another gains is when the state intervenes and creates a monopoly. Then the market fails to operate and somebody may be aggrandized, while another is impoverished. But that is contrary to the whole concept of free market economics. I suppose there are few things in our time more denigrated than this whole concept of free enterprise, or market economy, or as our adversaries pejoratively call it, *capitalism*. My friend, is capitalism the great source of evil in the world today or is it one of God's great benefactions to mankind?

THE FREE MARKET AND ECONOMIC GROWTH

Adam Smith wrote his famous foundational work, *The Wealth of Nations*, in 1776, the birthday of America. We were, in a way, born together. Though the Bible laid out some of the principles upon which such a free system should be built, people never put them all together. The Reformers, particularly Calvin, helped to bring many of them to light. On that basis Adam Smith finally put the pieces together in his book. This has impelled scholars to say that around 1780, modern capitalism began.

In 1780, four-fifths of the French expended 90 percent

of their income on food, with only what you and I consider a marginal tip to a waitress. They had yet to provide for all their other needs. In that same year in Germany, less than 1,000 people earned $1,000 a year or more. Europe had been in like condition for thousands of years. In 1780, Europe was little different than modern Africa, with the vast majority of people living on subsistence wages, eking out an existence from hand-to-mouth. At last, scriptural principles, re-enunciated by the reformers, were put into place and took effect. From 1800 to 1850, with inflation out of the picture, real wages quadrupled. From 1850 to 1900, real wages (after inflation) quadrupled again, so that in the nineteenth century, actual wealth and income increased sixteen times over. The world had never seen anything like that before! This was true in England, and it was even truer in America, where free enterprise had its freest reign.

Nevertheless, the statist concepts began marching once again, and the socialist utopians began to weave their magic spells over people's minds. The old idea of "something for nothing" permeated thought and desire, until it increasingly interfered with the type of economic system that had made America into the land of plenty and opportunity. As a consequence, today we have enormous economic problems, and we "hop along with one foot tied up behind our back," so to speak.

For example, in 1982, $283.9 billion was taken from one group of people and given to another. These monies are called *transfer payments*.[1] These transfer payments are made in the name of "social justice," in the name of a "static economic pie," and in the name of an "equitable redistribution of wealth." What is not acknowledged is that the free enterprise system, as clearly outlined in the Scripture, provides for economic expansion and for priority being placed on production, rather than simply on the distribution of scarce resources. Consider with me a few of the results of this system today.

WHAT A WELFARE STATE BRINGS

The welfare state inevitably produces more of that which it sets out to cure. In 1948, there were practically no transfer payments in this country. Now a huge proportion of our population is poverty-stricken, and they receive government assistance in increasing numbers. Anything the government subsidizes, it produces more of. If chickens are selling for a dollar a pound and the government subsidizes them for a dollar fifty a pound, what inevitably happens? In five years, you are up to your armpits in chickens! The same is true with the welfare system. We are going to have more and more people on it.

It has famously been said that "America will last until the populace discovers that it can vote for itself largesse out of the public treasury." "Largesse" is a term any sixth grader reading *McGuffey's Reader* would know. The average American today with a public school education probably does not know what the term means—"to vote for themselves gifts or handouts from the public treasury." America will last until the public discovers that it can do just that! Now the majority of the public has discovered it with a vengeance, and the politicians are bending over backwards to let the remainder know. It is coming on like a locomotive. People are wondering what they can get out of the federal government, and they believe they have a *right* to it. They are demanding it! Politicians can buy votes by giving away other people's money.

The welfare state creates a desire in people to take advantage of public monies. Those on welfare expect to be cared for and will ever want more. Those not on welfare will grow envious and desire, if not to be completely supported, to be helped for their own selfish ends. The few who work will become discouraged. They will see that work is unnecessary or undesirable for earning a living. When people no longer desire to work, or to work hard, the whole system will collapse.

The welfare state inevitably produces conflict. Recently, after the President spoke, a group of protesters were interviewed. Every one of them was angrier than a hornet because each wanted more money out of the public treasury for his little thing, whatever it was. "We want money for this, and we want money for that. Give me! Give me! Give me!" Every segment of society will be at the other's throats until society degenerates into rancor, riots, and ultimately anarchy. What else could you expect when a government expropriates a huge pot of money and doles it out, not to those most in need, but to those who apply the greatest political pressure? The ultimate beneficiaries, however, are not the intended recipients, but the bureaucrats who administer it.

Why is it that one county in Maryland and another one in Virginia, which are the two bedroom-counties for Washington, D.C., have the highest per capita income in the United States? These counties are where the bureaucrats live. Why is it that we give $30,000 per person for those living on tribal lands administered by the Bureau of Indian Affairs, and those living there can still barely scratch out a living? Well, the people in the Bureau of Indian Affairs are doing just fine, thank you.

Public charity, charity dispensed by the state, leads to vice and indolence. It is well known that private charity discriminates. It takes into consideration the lifestyle and the worthiness of the individual. For example, the twenty-two-year-old who is living at home and loses his job, and is dependent upon his parents, and does not go out and look for a job, won't sit around idly and twiddle his thumbs for the next nine months. His parents will soon have him out on the street pounding the pavement and looking for work. When the Federal Government dispenses charity, however, it is a nice time for a holiday. Let's go to Florida! Private charity encourages thrift and virtue. Public charity engenders immorality and indolence. The more you pay for illegitimate children, the more illegitimate children you are going to have. It is a basic rule of economics.

Public charity and the welfare state destroy private charity. Last year 283 billion dollars were expropriated from citizens and distributed to others—that money was unavailable for private charity. Just think what could have been done! There are those who would criticize the private charities for not doing more. Yet when all of these assets are taken by the government, it leaves charities with precious little to do anything with.

SPIRITUAL CONSEQUENCES

All this leads to *statism* and *unbelief*. Instead of drawing people to the church and to God, (who is the provider of every good and perfect gift), a welfare state leads more and more to a secularized state, and it engenders more and more unbelief in the populace. Furthermore, it leads to a loss of freedom and to tyranny, as we sell our souls to the government store. More and more people are willing to sell their birthright for "a mess of pottage," or as someone said, "a pot of socialistic message." Such people end up totally dependent upon the state and devoid of liberty.

The meaning of life is lost. The socialist says that this is all the life there is. You only go around once; therefore, the things in this life are the only things that count, and no one must be allowed to fail. This is the only life there is, and to fail here is to fail ultimately and totally and finally and forever. The Christian says that this is a probation that is going to lead to everlasting life in heaven or hell. How we exercise this probation is going to determine what happens to us there.

Therefore, every person must have an opportunity to succeed or fail. The socialist totally denies this because of his materialistic and atheistic view of life. He hinders God's purpose for life and destroys all meaning and significance. That is why Sweden, the most socialized of Western nations, has the highest suicide rate in the world. That is why the Soviet Union has the highest alcohol consumption in the world. Though all of the bread for life has been provided by the government, life itself has lost all of its significance and is no longer worth living.

THE ONE THING WE DON'T HAVE TO WORK FOR

God says that if anyone will not work, he should not eat. Yet, there is one thing we cannot work for—eternal life! We cannot obtain it by our own abilities. This is the only free gift available to man. Tragically, people turn this upside down. They try to make *this* life free and ignore the *next*, but God says we are to work in this life, and the gift of everlasting life is by the grace of God alone—paid for by Jesus Christ.

We can grow petunias or turnips, but when it comes to a sunset, God says, "Step aside. This is a job for the Almighty." We can run a church or preach a sermon, but when it comes to the eternal salvation of mankind, God says, "Step aside. This is a job for the Divine Redeemer."

We need to trust in Him and receive the free gift of eternal life. We need to receive His meaning and significance and purpose for our lives and work with our hands, doing that which is good. We should accumulate the things of this world *so that* we may have to give, as the Scripture says, unto those who are in need. Then charity and compassion will abound toward those who lack the physical things of this life, and in this, Christ will be honored and His kingdom will spread.

Let us ask our heavenly Father, whose Word contains truths for every area of our lives, to make us men and women who are faithful and strong and obedient and true to Him. Let us also pray for our nation that it will turn its heart back unto Him, so that He will again restore the prosperity that can only come from obedience to His laws!

---

1   In *Lord of All*, (2005), D. James Kennedy and Jerry Newcombe noted that *transfer payments* (defined as money given by the government to it citizens) had increased to nearly a trillion dollars. They calculated this figure by adding the amount that was being distributed through food assistance programs, public health service, health care financing, the housing and urban development department, unemployment benefits and the Social Security Administration (p. 154). Current bailouts to various selected sectors of America's business community could also be classified as *transfer payments*.

CHAPTER TWO

THE CHRISTIAN VIEW OF ECONOMICS*

*Is there a Christian view of economics?
Can we go to the Bible to find information that
will help us in these present difficult times?*

*As we saw in the previous chapter, Dr. Kennedy pointed out that
the Bible has a great deal to say about what is true and valuable.
It affirms both the value of work and the responsibility we all have
to use our economic resources to demonstrate our honesty and
our charity. In this chapter, preached 20 years after the
message in chapter one, Dr. Kennedy returns to these
principles and elaborates on them, giving us added
understanding of their importance and their
current application.*

* This was originally preached by Dr. D. James Kennedy at Coral Ridge
Presbyterian Church in Fort Lauderdale, Florida, on May 25, 2003.

> *"But Peter said, 'Ananias, why has Satan filled your
> heart to lie to the Holy Spirit and keep back part
> of the price of the land for yourself?'"*
> *—Acts 5:3*

On Memorial Day we remember those who have struggled and fought and even died for America. But what have they fought for? They have fought for freedom. What does that mean? Well, they have fought for political freedom, they have fought for religious freedom, and they have fought for economic freedom—the things that make America great.

All of those freedoms are still under attack in our nation today, however. Even though America became a free nation several centuries ago, there are those in this country who have worked and are still working to try to undermine that political freedom. There are those that would like to see our autonomy and our freedom turned over to someone else, namely the United Nations.

Many people don't realize that this has come closer than you might think. A bill was passed by our Congress—a bill that would have allowed the World Court of the United Nations to have direct jurisdiction over any one of you whom they chose to bring before them. This court is made up of people who, for the most part, do not share the values and the godly principles that make up this nation. However, an amendment was passed that now protects you from this ungodly court and prevents them from snatching you out of this country, away from the protections of our Constitution, in order to try you before them in some foreign country.

Religious freedom! We thought we had attained it, and yet, for the last century there have been those who have not ceased to try to undermine it. They are like termites, and step-by-step, little by little, they have taken away one piece after another of our religious freedom. Even now the ACLU and all its friends continue to do just that.

Not only is America the land of the free; it is the land of opportunity. It is "a city set on a hill," a city of gold in the eyes of a lot of people. Many in foreign countries think that the streets in America are paved with gold—that this is the wealthiest nation in the world, and if they could just get here, they might, indeed, realize their economic dreams. There are those, however, who are working to undermine our economic freedom as well.

It is not merely coincidental, but quite providential, that in the birth year of this nation, a very significant book was written by Adam Smith entitled *The Wealth of Nations*. Smith was a professor of moral philosophy at Glasgow University, which was a Puritan university at the time. In his book he described what is known as the *free enterprise system*, or as it is sometimes called, *capitalism*. Significantly, Smith's book was published in the very year of the Declaration of Independence—1776.

Several centuries before, John Calvin gave us the first glimmers of a free enterprise kind of system. Since all of the Puritans and Pilgrims who came to these shores were followers of Calvin, they already knew a good deal about that system. But Smith "connected the dots" and gave us a full-fledged system. Therefore, the *age of capitalism* is dated by historians from the publication of Smith's book.

Again, there are those that would try to do away with our free enterprise system. In 1948, the liberal World Council of Churches was formed in Amsterdam. At the very first meeting, they called upon Christians all over the world to abandon capitalism and adopt *socialism*. They started Christian social organizations. They called for *social justice*, and many liberal churches followed in their train and began to proclaim those views that encouraged socialism. Of course, they also declared that socialism was taught in the Bible.

SOCIALISM

Is it? Let us go right to the citadel of this view and take a look at Acts 4. Here we read,

. . . neither did anyone say that any of the things

he possessed was his own, but they had all things in common. . . . Nor was there anyone among them who lacked; for all who were possessors of lands or houses sold them, and brought the proceeds of the things that were sold, and laid *them* at the apostles' feet; and they distributed to each as anyone had need.

—Acts 4:32, 34-35

Now this might actually sound like socialism, or even communism—"From each according to his ability to each according to his need." But a "text without a context is a pretext." These verses, joined together and taken out of their context, have served as a pretext to sell a "mess of socialistic pottage" to millions of Christians in America and around the world.

THE CONTEXT OF ACTS 4:32 & 34-35

The context of these verses is found in the following few verses. In Acts 5:1, we read that Ananias and Sapphira had a piece of land, and they sold it and brought *part* of the money and laid it at the apostles' feet. But Peter said, "Ananias, why has Satan filled your heart to lie to the Holy Spirit and keep back *part* of the price of the land for yourself?" (Acts 5:3).

Keep in mind, one of the most basic and primary tenets of both *socialism* and *communism* is that the state either owns property and the means of production, or at least controls them. In fact, a well known Parisian socialist, Proudhon, is famous for a brief statement that has been repeated millions of times in the writings of socialists—his definition of property. Do you know how he defined it? "Property," said Proudhon, "is theft." That is socialism—"Property is theft!" Do you think that you own private property? There is no such thing, according to Proudhon's definition. It belongs to everyone. It is the people's property and is owned and cared for on their behalf by the state, which somehow or other always manages to keep most of it for itself.

But what does the Scripture say? It says, "While it remained, was it not your own?" (Acts 5:4). This is private property—the very antithesis of both socialism and communism. For us to exercise our responsibilities before God, both of justice and of charity, it is essential that we own property. Therefore, God guards private property with the flaming sword of his own commandment, "You shall not steal" (Exodus 20:15)—a divine guarantee of private property.

"And after it was sold," said Peter, "was it not in your own control?" (Acts 5:4). Even the results of the sale of his property were not controlled by the state, but were in Ananias' own power. This undermines another tenet of communism and socialism. Furthermore, we read that various disciples, including Barnabas and others, sold their property and brought the money and laid it at the feet of Pontius Pilate. . . . No! They laid it at the feet of the *apostles*! There is nothing in this world that would be a greater abomination to Marx, Engels, Stalin, and Lenin than the idea that people would give their property to the *Church*. They wanted to destroy the Church, not enrich it! But that is what the early Christians did. Again, another pillar of socialism and communism is undermined.

VOLUNTARY VERSUS INVOLUNTARY

Finally, in this section of Acts we also have the *coup de grâce*, the death blow, to the whole communist-socialist undertaking. They "brought the proceeds of the things that were sold, and laid *them* at the apostles' feet" (Acts 4:35) *voluntarily*. Communism and socialism enforce *in*voluntary actions by the power of the state. But what the early Christians did was purely voluntary.

I have not the slightest objection to any Christians anywhere getting together and deciding to establish a Christian commune and having all of their property in common and sharing everything they have. I have no objection to that, whatsoever. I will say, however, that I would not be too optimistic about the results, since this has been tried over and over again and has always failed. But that is certainly their prerogative—because it is voluntary. Socialism and communism operate with the sword of the state. That is not voluntary at all!

Notice that this was never commanded by God—neither in this passage nor anywhere else in the Bible. Out of the exuberance of the outpouring of the Holy Spirit and the tremendous feelings of love they had, they *wanted* to do it. They wanted to share with one another. It was purely voluntary, so instead of teaching socialism or communism, this example is the very antithesis. It is a body blow to everything that socialism and communism hold dear.

ARE SOCIALISM AND COMMUNISM DIFFERENT?

Many try to say there is a great difference between communism and socialism. Socialism may be established in one of two ways. It may be established suddenly and violently by force—as when the Russian revolution established the USSR. Or it may be established slowly and gradually—as the Fabian Socialists have recommended in England. But both are still socialism.

It is significant that the media have tried over many decades to show that communism is at one end of the spectrum and Nazism is at the other. Communism is the far left. Nazism, we are told, is the far right. What they like to say is that Nazism was conservative and communism was liberal, and then they equate American conservatives with the Nazis.

This is a fabric of lies. What does "Nazi" mean? It stands for the "National *Socialist* Party." What did "USSR" stand for? It is the "Union of Soviet *Socialist* Republics." Communism and Nazism and socialism are *all* on the left. Communism is simply one form of socialism. Both have generally bankrupted or impoverished the nations where they have been tried.

THE PILGRIM'S SOCIALIST EXPERIMENT

You may remember that America began as a socialist nation. When the Pilgrims landed, they had a socialist economy—but not of their own doing. It was forced upon them by the London Company, which had provided the money for them to undertake their venture. What were the results? Fifty percent of the Pilgrims died the first year, and most of the remainder were so near starvation that they almost all perished.

Finally, (as Governor Bradford noted in his diaries), they realized that they had tried to be "wiser than God," and they now understood the "folly" of this experiment. They abandoned it completely, gave to every person a piece of his own private land, and encouraged each of them to work it. The result was absolutely startling! The people were energized. They got out and worked diligently, and soon they were rejoicing in thanksgiving. Somehow this message doesn't get out very clearly in our schools today—but we need to remember that this socialist fiasco almost destroyed our nation in its infancy.

Socialism has had a disastrous effect everywhere it exists. The reason it failed among the Pilgrims is because they forgot that man—even regenerated man, even the new man in Christ, even a born-anew Christian—still has much of the old nature left in him. That nature is selfish. It is inclined to sloth, and it is inclined to try to get out of as much work as possible. Therefore, socialism will not work anywhere in the world.

In America we have not had a revolution. We have not had a violent explosion like the Soviet Union, but we have been following the Fabian Socialist plan of a step-by-step, incremental abandonment of capitalism, and a steady movement toward socialism.

STEP ONE: WIN THE BATTLE OF SEMANTICS

In any war, before the first battle is fought, the semantic battle needs to be won. That is always the way it is; it doesn't matter where. Before the Nazis could kill the Jews, the courts in Germany declared that Jews were "non-persons." In our country, slavery was affirmed when the Supreme Court declared in the *Dred Scott* decision that the slave could never be a citizen and was considered "property," not a person.

In the abortion war, the abortionists early realized the power of semantics. They immediately claimed the high semantic ground by using the term *pro-choice*. How many millions have unthinkingly accepted that term! But consider this—through all of America's existence, have any women ever been prevented from carrying their children to term and giving birth? How many societies, how many political movements were formed to enable women to be able to carry their children and give birth? Not one! The only "choice" the pro-choice people have is the choice of death. The other choice has always been there, but they don't acknowledge it.

The semantic battle has also been fought in the case of socialism. We saw earlier that the liberals called for a "Christian socialism." Then they called for *social justice*. Now almost everything that goes on in Washington today is based on the concept of social justice. But how many people can define it, much less compare justice to charity? However, these two are antithetical—they are virtually opposites.

JUSTICE

Interestingly, the famous statue of Lady Justice has three very obvious features that define justice quite aptly. If you've seen a picture of this statue, you will recall that the first thing we notice is that she is *blindfolded*. This reminds us that justice is blind; it *does not discriminate*. It doesn't matter whether you are young or old, black or white, tall or short, fat or thin, rich or poor, justice is the same for all, and thus it should be.

Second, Lady Justice has a pair of *balanced scales* in her left hand, reminding us that justice is *equitable*—it is equal for all. There is equal justice for all under the law, we say, and thus it should be.

Third, what does Justice have in her right hand? A *sword*— and what is the sword the symbol of? It is the symbol of the state; it is the symbol of *coercion*. The Bible says that the magistrate, the state "does not bear the sword in vain" (Romans 13:4). It is the power of coercion all the way to the taking of life. This is what the statue represents, and here is a perfect definition of justice: it is *non-discriminating*; it is perfectly *fair and balanced*, and it is *enforced* by the state—it is *involuntary*.

Imagine that you have been taken into court and accused of murder. The trial has taken place, and you have been found guilty. Now you have been sentenced to die in the electric chair. You stand up and say, "I have had just about enough of this. I am not going to have anything more to do with your faulty legal system"—and you walk out of the court. Would that ever happen? No—you would not even get to the door of the courtroom. Your presence there is involuntary.

Some say that paying taxes is voluntary and have tried to

test this out. Most of them can be reached at the penitentiary. They have found out that it's not true. Taxation is an involuntary system.

CHARITY

Charity, on the other hand, is the opposite of everything I have just described. Charity is not blind. It sees. It *discriminates*, as do all of us in our charity. We see something that we believe is worthy of our support, and we support it. But that doesn't mean that we support everything we see. Have you supported *every* cause and *every* person who has ever come to you and asked for money? You have given to *some*, but you have not given to *all*. The Scripture says, "Is it not lawful for me to do what I wish with my own things?" (Matthew 20:15). Of course it is, for charity discriminates. It weighs the good and the bad.

Today we live in a society where some are trying to take discrimination out of those areas where it is proper, as in personal charity, and make it hold for everything. The result is that no one is able to discriminate any longer between good and evil, worth and non-worth, value and non-value. If a universal principle of *nondiscrimination* is carried through all parts of our society, it will produce absolute chaos.

The essence of charity is that it is *voluntary*. No money that is extracted from you at the point of a sword, whether it's the sword of Robin Hood or the sword of the state, can be counted as charity, because it is *in*voluntary. There is a vast difference between the *state* taking your money and giving it to others and *your* giving it!

WHAT IS FAIR?

Furthermore, charity is not based upon *fairness*. You don't give the same amount to all. You give to some and not to others, because it is yours to give. It is not coerced. You do it voluntarily.

Many people don't recognize what is happening today in regard to people's attitudes about *fairness*. Someone described it this way:

Fifty-thousand people bought tickets to a baseball game, but the game was rained out, and the crowd is due to receive a refund. As the team is about to mail out the refunds, the congressional liberals stop them and suggest that they send out refunds based upon the liberal national committee's interpretation of *fairness*. After all, if the refunds are made based on the price each person paid for a ticket, most of the money would go to the wealthiest ticket holders. That would be unconscionable!

- Therefore, people in the $10 seats would get back $15, because they couldn't afford the better seats. Call it an "Earned Income Ticket Credit." (Oh, it's wonderful to win the semantic wars!) "Earned" in this case means that the person has demonstrated *less* ambition, *less* skills and *poorer* work habits, thus keeping him or her at low entry-level wages.
- People in the $15 seats would get back $15, because that's only "fair"—according to whom? According to the liberal committee.
- People in the $25 seats would get back $1, because they already make a lot of money and don't need a refund. If they can afford a $25 ticket, they must not be paying enough taxes.
- People in the $50 luxury seats will get back nothing. In fact, they will have to pay an additional $50, because it is obvious that they have way too much money to spend already.
- People driving by the stadium who couldn't afford to even watch the game will get $10 each, even though they didn't put anything in, because they need the most help.

Now do you understand "fairness?" Yet that is exactly the picture that is presented to us. On the front page of our paper yesterday, there was a statement about how much money different groups of people would receive from the recent tax cut. The purpose of the article was obvious—to show that this tax cut was "not fair." The people who made the most money got the most money back, the people who made less money got less money back, and the people that made the least money got very little money back. That is obviously not "fair," that is not "just," and obviously the newspaper was trying to make a point!

However, although this was portrayed not only in the local newspaper, but also by various news organizations, the one thing I've never seen on the front page of our paper is a breakdown of how much taxes these various income groups pay. The top five percent of the income earners in this country make about 35 percent of the total income in America. "Fairness" would dictate that they pay 35 percent. They are actually paying 56 percent, and this is going up. Over the last several decades, the shift in the amount of taxes paid has been rising substantially for the higher levels of income, which becomes *confiscatory taxation*.

On the other hand, the lower 50 percent of the wage earners in this country earn only 13 percent of the total income in this nation. "Fairness" would dictate that they certainly shouldn't pay any more than 13 percent. How much do they pay? 3.9 percent. If we want to be fair, we will greatly lessen the taxes on the top 5 percent and increase them on the others.

We should not call this "unfair" or "unjust." We should recognize it for what it is. It is a *transfer payment*—taking money from some people and giving it to other people. This is going a long way down the Fabian stepladder into *socialism*. How far down? Let me say that we now have a national budget of about $2 trillion. Almost $1 trillion of that is made up of transfer payments, where money is taken from you and given to him or taken from her and given to them. So we are a long way toward socialism in this country. The more this happens in any nation, the more it reduces the total productivity of that nation. And the evils produced by socialism are many, including indolence, unbelief, materialism, and a loss of the meaning of life.

The Bible is right! "If anyone will not work, neither shall he eat" (II Thessalonians 3:10). Many of us might find this to be a harsh statement, but this is truly the most compassionate statement about economics ever made—it was made by our compassionate God. Notice it doesn't say, "anyone *who cannot* work," or "anyone who is *not able* to work," but rather, "If anyone *will not* work, neither shall he eat." Following this command would do more for the economic well-being of more people than almost anything else we could do! Then, through private charity, those who work would be able to help more people in more beneficial ways than any socialist state could ever do.

The Bible teaches the very antithesis of socialism—it teaches that God is the center of our lives and of our world, and that we should live according to His teachings. Let us pray that He will cause this nation to turn away from its greed and covetousness, where everyone is crying "I want mine," "I want mine," "I want mine," and that He would restore our nation to the system of freedom—political, religious, *and* economic—that made this nation great.

CHAPTER THREE

DOES THE BIBLE TEACH SOCIALISM?*

The themes in this chapter have been touched on in previous chapters. In this chapter, however, Dr. Kennedy makes a number of additional points on the nature of socialism in comparison to biblical principles of economics.

For example, he notes that the reason socialism is being embraced is that we've rejected biblical teaching in every sphere of life, and secular humanism has become the dominant worldview. Also, in the final section he elaborates on the breakdown caused in societies where socialism prevails. We trust that as you read this chapter, you will appreciate the additional insights it provides on the differences between biblical principles of economics and socialism.

* This was originally delivered by Dr. D. James Kennedy at Coral Ridge Presbyterian Church in Fort Lauderdale, Florida, on October 18, 1981.

> *But Peter said, "Ananias, why has Satan filled your heart
> to lie to the Holy Spirit and keep back part of the price
> of the land for yourself? While it remained, was it not your
> own? And after it was sold, was it not in your own
> control? Why have you conceived this thing in your heart?
> You have not lied to men but to God."*
> *—Acts 5:3, 4*

Secular humanism is the most fixed and implacable antagonist that Christianity faces in America today. It is particularly intractable in the sphere of our national government. We find that secular humanists continually stress the need for more and more socialism. Because they deny the existence of God, they obviously have no Creator and are thrown back on evolution. Because there is no God who is the eternal lawgiver, they are thrown into situational ethics and moral relativism. Because they do not believe there is a provident God to provide for the needs of His creation, they are also thrown onto the "provident state" to provide for the needs of people.

There are those in the Christian community who certainly lend aid and support to such thinking by saying that the Bible teaches socialism. There are also others who say that the Bible does not teach anything about economic matters at all, and that the Bible is not a textbook on economics. When you hear statements like, "The Bible is not a textbook on science," or "The Bible is not a textbook on economics or government," and so on, you should remember that the Bible is not a textbook on theology either. Rather, the Bible is a revelation of God's dealings with mankind in *all* spheres and activities in this world. The Bible gives us principles which apply to *every* phase of our lives.

The divinely given principles revealed in the Bible affect every facet of man's existence—whether they be theological, spiritual, governmental, scientific, historical, economic, or any other principles. When a person says the Bible is not a textbook for "such and such," what's really being said is that he or she rejects the broad principles the Bible lays down in a particular discipline. Because the Bible's guidance has been rejected in every sphere of human existence, millions of people today wander like mice in a maze. They are like people lost at sea in a ship without either a chart or compass. They know not whither they should go or even in which direction they should head.

SECULAR HUMANISTS EXTOL SOCIALISM

Having rejected biblical principles of economics, secular humanists continually extol *socialism*. They praise the virtues of Karl Marx and his view of the field of economics. They cite the need for America to abandon its *free enterprise system* in order to become socialized and collectivized. However, before we get into the secular humanist concept of socialism, let us answer the question: Does the Bible teach socialism?

Those who claim it does invariably appeal to the passage from Acts dealing with Ananias and Barnabas. Barnabas, you recall, sold a piece of land and brought the money and gave it to the apostles. Ananias and his wife also sold a piece of land, but kept back a part of the price. They brought only a portion of it to the apostles and lied about it. It is claimed that this passage contains within it all the basic principles of socialism. On the contrary, not only does this passage *not* teach the principles of socialism, it countermands all the fundamental tenets of socialism. In fact, it is an unparalleled broadside against the socialist ship of state. There is no more explicit repudiation of socialism than that which is found in this very passage.

Remember, the basic concept of socialism is that the *state* either owns or controls all *property*, or it controls the *means of production*. Whether the state owns the property or controls it, however, it ultimately makes very little difference. If you have a document that says you own these things, but you do not have the control or, if you do not have the fruits of production left to you, it is an empty document indeed! Just as one of the early French socialists, Proudhon, made his famous declaration that "property is theft," Marx and Engels and all the rest inveigh mightily against both private ownership and private control of the means of production.

THOU SHALT NOT STEAL

What does the Bible say? The Ten Commandments are a clear repudiation of this. The commandment, "You shall not steal" (Exodus 20:15), as virtually every theologian for twenty centuries has declared, is a divine guarantee of *private property*. I cannot steal something from you if you do not own it! Furthermore, in the Decalogue, we also have the command, "You shall not covet your neighbor's house; ... nor anything that is your neighbor's" (Exodus 20:17).

Does the New Testament change this? Is private property repudiated or is it taught in Acts 5? Notice what Peter said to Ananias, "While it remained, was it not your own?" (Acts 5:4). Is there a clearer statement of the ownership of property than that? While it remained . . . [Before you sold it . . .] Was it not your own? Did you not own it? Could you not do with it whatever you will? Even after you sold it, was not the money your own? Ananias had full control of all he had earned in the sale. The Bible clearly teaches the *right of private property*, because God has given the whole world unto mankind as a *stewardship*. It is ours to use with full responsibility before God.

Second, note that this action was *voluntary*. There was no commandment to sell or to give the funds away; they decided voluntarily to do so. Look at the context—there was "great grace upon them," and being so overwhelmed by the grace of God working mightily in their hearts, they did this out of the abundance of their concern. It was voluntarism. Nothing militates more strongly against modern concepts of socialism than *voluntarism*, for *coercion* lies at the heart of every socialistic scheme in modern centuries.

Third, consider the *disposition of the money*. They didn't lay it at the feet of Pontius Pilate; they didn't lay it at the feet of Caesar, or even give it to the local tax collector. The Bible says several times, "They laid it at the apostles' feet" (Acts 4:35, 37). Nothing would have given Karl Marx apoplexy more than the idea that people should sell all their property and give the money to the Church. That is antithetical to the whole spirit of modern socialism. Yet people have the temerity to say that this passage in Acts teaches modern state socialism. Nothing can be farther from the truth!

CONDITIONS FOR SUCCESS OF SOCIALISM

The great theologian, Charles Hodge, former Professor of Systematic Theology at Princeton Seminary, has said that the aims and purposes of the early Christians could not be farther from the schemes of modern adherents of socialism and communism than heaven is from the lower parts of the earth!

Furthermore, Hodge noted in regard to the schemes of socialism, "The conditions of the success of this plan, on any large scale, cannot be found on earth." Hodge elaborated,

> . . . It supposes that men will labour as assiduously without the stimulus of the desire to improve their condition to secure the welfare of their families as with it. It supposes absolute disinterestedness on the part of the more wealthy, the stronger, or the more able members of the community. They must be willing to forego all personal advantages from their superior endowments. It supposes perfect integrity on the part of the distributors of the common fund, and a spirit of moderation and contentment in each member of the community, to be satisfied with what others, and not he, may think to be his equitable share.[1]

What was Hodge's conclusion? "The attempt to introduce a general community of goods in the present state of the world, instead of elevating the poor, would reduce the whole mass of society to a common level of barbarism and poverty."[2]

AMERICA'S EARLY EXPERIMENT IN SOCIALISM

That is a pretty strong statement! Is it true? Would it or would it not? Well, we have seen in America a perfect, almost a laboratory, experiment showing whether or not this is true. Many people do not realize that America, the land of the free enterprise system, began with socialism. Were you aware of that fact? If not, then I commend to you Governor William Bradford's account of the story of Plymouth Plantation. The Pilgrims who landed at Plymouth determined that all things would be held in common and that people would work for the common good. That was in 1620, when they landed. The result was a tremendous crop failure in the first year—a most exiguous and meager production. Many people were hungry and many were starving. The following year another poor crop was produced. By that time, half of the Plymouth population had died.

Therefore, in 1623, Governor Bradford declared that henceforth, this experiment in a community of goods, a socialistic experiment, would be abandoned. Every man would receive a parcel of land of his own. Each would work it and take care of his own family. The result? People went to work with alacrity. Men who had feigned sickness were now eager to get into the fields. Even the women eagerly went out to work. Before then, the idea that any women should be told to work in the fields was thought to be the greatest tyranny. Now the women took their children with them and happily engaged in labor for the benefit of their own families. What was the result? The following harvest was tremendous and bountiful—and the first Thanksgiving was celebrated in America!

Note it well, my friends: When socialism was abandoned, Thanksgiving was established. When socialism is reestablished in America, "Thanksgiving" will be abolished. That is a lesson in the history of America that we need to learn.

THE DESTRUCTION OF AMERICAN CIVILIZATION

It has been said that America would only last until the people discover that they can vote for themselves *largesse* or public benefits out of the public treasury. Have the American people now learned this? Indeed, they have learned it with a vengeance! Furthermore, those who haven't yet discovered it are being pandered to by politicians who stand for nothing more than their own reelection. They pander to people's desire for the government to give them more and more and more. The result will be the destruction of American civilization. My friends, we are far advanced down that road today—farther along than most people realize.

The Breakdown of the Family

What are the adverse effects of this plunge into socialism as it relates to the teachings of the Word of God? First, it is *the breakdown of the family*, the basic unit of any civilization. As goes the family, so goes the nation. I do not know of anything more pernicious for the family life than the concept of a state welfare system. Ties that have for centuries bound the generations together have been completely severed.

There is a need, which the Bible addresses, for the care of people who cannot care for themselves—the care of infants and children, the care of the elderly, the care of the infirm and the sick. In the Scripture, that responsibility ever devolves upon the individual, the family, and the church, but *never on the state*! However, we have thrown off that responsibility and cast it upon the state. We have broken the bonds that bind the family together, and we have gone a long way toward the destruction of the basic unit of civilization in America. The Bible says, "But if anyone does not provide for his own, and especially for those of his household, he has denied the faith and is worse than an unbeliever" (1 Timothy 5:8). I think that Christian America needs to hear this very clearly today.

A Breakdown in the Church

Second, socialism and the welfare state bring about *a breakdown in the Church*. It has been seen in one country after another that where socialism goes up, the spiritual life in the Church goes down. What has happened in the countries where socialism has been rampant, such as Sweden or Great Britain? Spiritual life has dropped to almost zero. What has happened in Europe, where no more than five percent of the people attend church on any given Sunday, and spiritual life is at an all-time low? If you look at the laws existing in Sweden, you will see all sorts of socialist laws hindering the work of the Church of Jesus Christ.

If the state is going to control the means of production, the question has to be asked: What does the state feel should be done with basic resources? Will it use wood and concrete for the building of churches? Will that be a high priority? Will they use paper for the printing of Bibles? Will their time be used to train pastors and evangelists? If you look at any socialist state, you will get a very clear answer to these questions.

A Breakdown in Christian Charity

Third, socialism brings *a breakdown in Christian charity.* The great motivation for private charity that is given in the Bible is destroyed. One thing we ought to clearly understand—you will attain no moral or spiritual merit from giving that is coerced. The rich people Robin Hood robbed did not advance spiritually by having their goods confiscated and given to others. If there is no *motivation of voluntary giving,* there is no spiritual aspect to the deed. Today government in our country takes such a large portion of our income that there is little left for private charity.

An Adverse Effect Upon the Recipients

Fourth, there is *an adverse effect upon the recipients.* There are no greater victims of the welfare system than the welfare recipients themselves. As Christians, we need to perceive the fact that these people are being spiritually and financially destroyed by this system. They are being cut off from upward mobility because they have never learned to work and have no way to escape their dependence on welfare. What this is doing to them spiritually is incalculable! How can a person live a spiritual life before God, who has commanded him to work, when welfare keeps him from working?

God has declared that life is simply a proving ground—a testing ground for eternity. He has commanded us to fulfill His Cultural Mandate: to till the earth, to work, and to do the things that He has given us to do as His stewards. God holds us accountable for this—He has created us for the purpose of working and giving glory to Him through our work. The Bible clearly says "For even when we were with you, we commanded you this: If anyone will not work, neither shall he eat" (2

Thessalonians 3:10). In a welfare system, there are millions of people who have no need to do so.

Adverse Effects on Income Producers

Fifth, there are *adverse effects on the income producers.* Just as those who receive welfare have their initiative and desire to work removed, those who are giving the money to this cause also find that their initiative is diminished. I talked to people in September that told me that if they work any more this year, the government will take almost all they make, and so they are not even working. You see what that does to the productivity of the nation? It drops dramatically! As taxes have gone up and up, and more and more money is being given away, productivity of the nation declines. Do you know what the result is? Inflation!

There are two causes of *inflation*: one is the government printing too much money, and the other is too little productivity. When there is too much money chasing too few goods and services, inflation is the inevitable result. If the productivity of America were increased ten percent, inflation would disappear. That will not happen where the motivation to produce is being destroyed—where welfare recipients don't have to work, and income producers have an increasing percentage of their income taken away.

Adverse Spiritual Effects in Our Nation

The entire wealth of the nation is being confiscated by a government that is also causing all sorts of other adverse spiritual effects in our country. This lessens the ability of the entire nation to survive. No! The Bible does not teach socialism. The adverse effects of it over time are incalculable. What the Bible teaches is *freedom* and *responsibility* and *work*—yet all of these are jettisoned in the socialistic state, and the spiritual effects are inescapable.

People get things completely reversed. While many have lost the biblical concept of working to earn their daily bread, the erroneous concept that we can earn eternal life by working prevails everywhere! The Bible teaches that we are to work for the things of this life, but that we can never *earn* eternal life. The gift of God is eternal life through Jesus Christ our Lord, because He alone could pay for it. That, my friends, is *free*!

There may be no free lunch in this world, but thank God, the marriage feast of the Lamb is free and paid for by Christ—but at an incredible cost on the cross at Calvary. It is offered to all those who place their trust in Him and receive Him into their heart as Savior and Lord. When they do so, they will see that this life is but a probation. In this life we are called upon by God to work and to produce and to fulfill our probation, so that we may hear the Lord say, "Well *done*, good and faithful servant; you were faithful over a few things, I will make you ruler over many things. Enter into the joy of your lord" (Matthew 25:21).

1 Hodge, Charles, *Systematic Theology*, Vol. 3 (Grand Rapids, Mich.: Wm. B. Eerdmans Publishing Co., 1940), pp. 429-430.
2 Hodge, Charles, *Systematic Theology*, Vol. 3, p. 430.

CHAPTER FOUR

CHRISTIANITY AND THE FEDERAL DEFICIT*

As was noted in the introduction to the first chapter, many are saying that our present economic woes are equal only to those of the Great Depression or the inflationary time of the Carter administration. Yet, as we see in this sermon preached ten years ago, we faced the same problems of spiraling debt and fear of depression then as well.

What is tragic is that in the intervening years our nation has failed to heed the admonitions of Dr. Kennedy and others to put our economy back on track by adopting sound fiscal and economic policies and by turning to God in repentance and faith. Instead, we continue to turn further away from God. Not only is our country ignoring His commands regarding sanctity of life and marriage, but we are spending our grandchildren's inheritance to satisfy our desires for material things, and we are looking to the government—not God—to supply all our needs.

*This was originally preached by Dr. D. James Kennedy at Coral Ridge Presbyterian Church in Fort Lauderdale, Florida, on January 9, 1989.

> *"The* LORD *is my shepherd; I shall not want."*
> *—Psalm 23:1*

According to the great majority of commentators, the overriding problem facing our nation at this time and facing the administration and Congress is the problem of the spiraling out of control national debt.

There has been much analysis of the situation—but all of it without God. There has been a great deal of discussion—but none of it has considered His Word. There has been much effort to find the root of our problem—but the spiritual and moral aspects of it are not being discussed. I do believe that this spiraling out of control national debt is, in fact, the greatest problem facing our nation today from an economic point of view. But I also believe that this is basically a moral and spiritual problem, and it is not going to be solved unless it is solved on a spiritual basis.

To give you some idea of the proportion of the problem, the national debt has reached approximately $5.3 trillion. [Twenty years later, our gross national debt, $10.6 trillion, is now twice that figure.—Ed.] We're throwing around that number, however, without really understanding its magnitude. Just a few years ago we were thinking about the fact that the national debt will soon reach a trillion dollars. At the time, that seemed unheard of . . . unimaginable, even.

How much is a trillion dollars? Consider this: if you had gone into business when Jesus Christ was born—a business that was so unprofitable that every year you lost a million dollars a day, seven days a week, it would still take you 700 more years from today to lose a trillion dollars. Here's another picture: if you had a four-inch stack of $1,000 bills that would be one *million* dollars. A stack of $1,000 bills 300 feet high adds up to a *billion* dollars. It would take a stack of $1,000 bills 63 miles high to give you a *trillion* dollars!

THE REAL CAUSE OF THE PROBLEM

This is a problem of enormous consequence. However, most people reading the newspaper and listening to the news have not grasped the real cause of the problem, because they haven't looked at it from a biblical and spiritual point of view. Dr. Charles Wolfe has given a very penetrating analysis of the basic spiritual problem. According to Dr. Wolfe, it has three parts:

- First, the *unredeemed* or *unregenerate* man has virtually unlimited wants and desires for material things. There is no limit to what he wants. He wants, he wants, he wants. He wants everything!
- Second, because he is unregenerate and does not have the power of God helping him, his ability to produce and meet all his wants is severely limited.
- Third, as a consequence, he has very little real satisfaction in life. He is always looking for some way other than God to meet his many wants and needs. He may turn to crime. He may try to forget his problems by engaging in addictive behaviors—drugs, alcohol, pornography or gambling. Or he may just go the way of many who make their business their god and sell their soul to obtain all the material pleasures of this life.

THE REAL ANSWER TO THE PROBLEM

In contrast to the *unregenerate* man or woman, however, the one who is *redeemed*, the one who has been *regenerated* by the Spirit of God and has trusted in Jesus Christ for salvation, has found that—

- since Jesus Christ came into his heart,
- since he has been regenerated by the Holy Spirit,
- since he has placed his trust in Christ as his Savior,
- since he knows that he has been adopted into the

family of God,

- since he knows that the King of kings is his Father and has promised to provide all of his needs out of His riches in glory and will take us into a mansion in paradise,
- and since he knows that God has promised that He will never leave him nor forsake him—

he now finds that his once virtually unlimited wants have been greatly constricted. Now he no longer wants much of this world.

In addition, the redeemed man has been given an enhanced ability to meet his diminished wants because he has become a new creature in Jesus Christ. Does that make a difference? Absolutely! It makes a difference in every way. Why?

First, we are not worried and anxious, nor are we frustrated. We do not feel limited in our abilities. The Scripture tells us, "Be anxious for nothing," "God shall supply all your need" (Philippians 4:6, 19).

Second, we have the help of God, who gives us additional strength to perform our tasks. "But the Lord stood with me and strengthened me" (II Timothy 4:17).

Third, we have new wisdom and ideas that come from God. "If any of you lacks wisdom, let him ask of God, who gives to all liberally and without reproach, and it will be given to him" (James 1:5).

Fourth, the one who's been redeemed is given the power to persevere and continue on when others may fall to the side. "Though he fall, he shall not be utterly cast down; For the LORD upholds *him with* His hand," (Psalm 37:24).

Fifth, we have a purpose in what we're doing. "For we are His workmanship, created in Christ Jesus for good works, which God prepared beforehand that we should walk in them" (Ephesians 2:10). Our work, whatever that may be, is done to the glory of God—"Excellence in all things, and all things for the glory of God."

PURITAN WORK ETHIC

There is a name for the five concepts I just presented.

Most people in America probably don't know what it is. It's the *Puritan Work Ethic*, or the *Protestant Work Ethic*. It has been virtually forgotten in America, and as a consequence we have seen a tremendous decline in our national productivity. These Christian concepts have been educated right out of the American people by way of our secularized humanistic education system in our government schools.

Because the redeemed man has been given these enhanced abilities, he actually produces more than he even wants of the world's goods. Therefore, he is enabled to give far more, he is enabled to save far more, and he is enabled to invest in more tools. A hundred years after the founding of our country, Americans were saving more than any people in the world and were investing more in tools. Americans had more tools than any nation and enjoyed the highest standard of living in the world.

That is no longer true. Today Americans *save less* than any other industrialized nation and *invest less* than any other industrialized nation. Our standard of living is no longer the highest in the world—and it is going down. Think of what our national debt will be when our children and grandchildren come of age.

SPENDING OUR GRANDCHILDREN'S INHERITANCE

The Bible says that inheritances should go from the fathers unto the sons, but we have reversed that concept. We are taking from our sons *and* our grandsons and are wasting it on our own immediate wants. We have lost the biblical concept of self-discipline—of saving and postponing the fulfillment of desires. We want our grandchildren to pay for the high standard of living that we are enjoying today. What we are doing to our grandchildren is so criminal that I wouldn't be at all surprised if the younger generation today says, when it reaches maturity, "Phooey on the whole bunch of you!" and just cuts us all off. We have already robbed them poor, and it is getting worse every day.

The Apostle Paul said, "I know how to be abased, and I know how to abound" (Philippians 4:12). Can you say that? Which describes you—the unregenerate or the regenerate, the unredeemed or the redeemed person? Are your material desires and wants almost unlimited, or are those material wants being limited more and more? Are you dissatisfied with your lot, or are you satisfied and content in your life?

"The LORD is my shepherd, I shall not want." What does the word "want" mean? It means "to lack, to have need of." "I shall not lack; I shall not have need." But then "want" also came to mean "to wish for that which is lacking, to desire." But if the Lord Jehovah is our Shepherd, we "shall not want." We shall neither lack nor shall we desire greatly the things of this world, because our God will supply all of our needs "according to His riches in glory by Christ Jesus" (Philippians 4:19).

THE WELFARE STATE

An unknown author described the problem very well in the following:

The Welfare State
The Government is my shepherd: I need not work.
It alloweth me to lie down on a good job;
It leadeth me beside still factories;
It destroyeth my initiative.
It leadeth me in the path of a parasite for politics sake;
Yes, though I walk through the valley of laziness and deficit spending,
I will fear no evil, for the government is with me.
It prepareth an economic Utopia for me, by appropriating the earnings of my own grandchildren.
It filleth my head with false security;
My inefficiency runneth over.
Surely the government should care for me all the days of my life,
And I shall dwell in the fool's paradise forever.

How tragically true this is. We call it the *welfare state* today. That is simply a euphemism for what is otherwise known as *socialism*. But some will say, "Doesn't the Bible teach that kind of thing? What about Acts 4 and 5, where we are told the Christians sold what they had and they brought it, they gave it, and they had all things in common. Isn't that teaching socialism—the welfare state?"

My friends, read Acts 4 and 5 carefully, and you will find that nothing could possibly repudiate socialism any more thoroughly than this passage does.

First, *they gave it to the church.* They sold their property and they brought all of the money and laid it at the feet of the *Apostles.*

Second, *their action was voluntary.* As Winston Churchill said, "Capitalism is the unequal distribution of wealth. Socialism is the equal distribution of poverty. Communism is [nothing but] socialism with a gun at [our] back." But the gun is there in socialism also. The power may have been gained at the ballot box, but appropriating the goods of one person and giving them to another is "a gun at your back." If you doubt it, just withhold it, and you will soon find out how true that is!

Third, Acts 5 *guarantees private property.* "While it remained, was it not your own? And after it was sold, was it not in your own control?" (Acts 5:4).

Finally, we see that *they were not following any command or injunction.* They acted out of the enthusiasm of the beginning of the Christian era and the outpouring of God's Spirit.

WHAT ABOUT THE POOR?

The question arises, "Shouldn't we be concerned for the poor?" Absolutely! That is why families, private charities, and community groups that are concerned about helping people in need have always been the way America has solved this problem. We have done this for almost 300 years, but now we are trying something else.

In his book, *Losing Ground,* sociologist Charles Murray points out what has happened since the time of President Johnson's Great Society in the early '60s. Murray uses exhaustive data to show that "We tried to provide more for the poor and [instead] produced more poor." As a *Christianity Today* review of *Losing Ground* says, "The real shocker in Murray's argument, however, is not that anti-poverty programs failed to eradicate poverty, but that they actually made things worse."

How could that possibly be? The black economist Walter Williams says this,

> We forgot that poor people are poor *but they're not stupid.* Poor people respond to economic incentives just like the rest of us. . . . Welfare has had devastating effects on the black family. In 1960, 20 percent of black children lived in father-absent households; today it is nearly 60 percent.

The poverty programs of the federal government of this country have virtually demolished the black family and are doing the same to poor white families. These programs have produced a whole generation of children who live in father-absent households. This has had a devastating effect on the very people that were supposed to be helped.

GOVERNMENT SUBSIDIES

How could this happen? Because the federal government forgot a very simple elementary economic principle—whatever the government subsidizes will increase! Just look back to the '30s, when pigs were subsidized. What was the result? There were so many pigs in America that tens of thousands were eventually shot and pushed into ditches. Corn, too, was subsidized. We produced so much corn that we didn't have any place to store it.

Now we're *subsidizing* illegitimate children. We have so many illegitimate children we don't know what to do with them. The same principle still applies—whatever the government subsidizes will increase.

A lady came up to me after I preached this in the first service and said, "I completely disagree with you."

"What do you disagree with?" I asked.

She said, "I believe we are our brother's keeper."

I said, "I completely agree with you. I believe we are, too. The difference between you and me is that I believe *we* are our brother's keeper, and you believe that the *government* is our brother's keeper." Her mouth fell open, and she walked away without saying another word.

A BUCKET WITH HOLES IN IT

Yes, we should help people—churches, charities, and private organizations are all expected to help people. However, when these institutions give help, it does not have the devastating effect of government welfare. What we must do is train people, so they won't become continual recipients of welfare, which has destroyed the incentive and the meaning of life for whole generations. Yet this is happening in our country today—not to mention the fact that escalating welfare is causing a federal deficit that is absolutely going to destroy America.

Ronald H. Nash has said,

> Most of the tax dollars collected to fight poverty end up . . . in the pockets of highly paid administrators, consultants, and staff as well as higher-income recipients of benefits from programs advertised as anti-poverty efforts. Clearly, the bucket used to carry money from the pockets of the taxpayer to the poor is leaking badly.

Nash points out that this is like taking a bucket of water to put out a fire—and then finding that the bucket has all sorts of holes in it! You run fifty feet to throw it on the fire and by the time you reach the fire, most of the water has leaked out. As Peter C. Peterson, former U.S. Secretary of Commerce has pointed out, even the majority of money that gets to anyone beyond the government administration goes to middle-class people and does not reach those for whom it is intended.

WHO IS RESPONSIBLE?

Who is to blame for all of this? Shall we blame it on the president? It has often been said that all spending programs begin in the House of Representatives. Shall we blame it on the

House of Representatives? No, my friends, I don't think we can. These officials are elected by people who vote for the person who has promised to give them the most federal monies.

Someone said in the early nineteenth century that, "America will last until the populace discovers that it can vote for itself largesse out of the public treasury." The problem we're facing today is the result of the greed and cupidity of the people of this country—and probably all of us here are receiving some sort of benefit as well. Only when the Spirit of God so works in our hearts that the things of this world and our desire for them is limited—only when our trust no longer is in government as our shepherd, but in our God—who has promised to provide all things—only when we get back to the Protestant (biblical) work ethic that provides for the material needs, the tools, the savings, and the investments that make for a prosperous nation—*only then* is there any hope of overcoming this problem.

David wrote, "The LORD is my shepherd, I shall not want." Jesus Christ said, "Beware of covetousness." The Apostle Paul declared, "I have learned in whatsoever state I am, therewith to be content." Can you declare this too?

Jesus Christ can give us a new perspective on *all* of life. He can enable us to see the ephemeral nature of the material things of this world—to see that those things that *are seen* are perishing, and those things that *are not seen* will never perish! May we seek His help to trust in Him as our Savior *and* Redeemer: so that we may be redeemed from the lust of material things, so that our affections may be fixed on things above, and so that we may be concerned for the *kingdom of God*—seeking first that kingdom and its righteousness, knowing that all these things shall be added unto us.

CHAPTER FIVE

GIVE ME, GIVE ME, GIVE ME!*

In 2005, Fort Lauderdale experienced a direct hit by hurricane Wilma—the first such occurrence in over forty years of Dr. Kennedy's ministry at Coral Ridge Presbyterian Church. Some of the church's roofing was blown away and water damaged the sanctuary. On November 6, less than two weeks after the hurricane had caused over 20 billion dollars worth of damage to Florida, Dr. Kennedy preached the following sermon to his congregation as they met in the church's fellowship hall. In this context he issued a challenge not to succumb to the attitude that now prevails in our society— "Give me, give me, give me!"

---

* This was originally preached by Dr. D. James Kennedy at Coral Ridge Presbyterian Church in Fort Lauderdale, Florida, on November 6, 2005.

> *"And the younger of them said to his father,*
> *'Father, give me the portion of goods that falls*
> *to me.' So he divided to them his livelihood."*
> —Luke 15:12

It has been called the greatest short story ever written, and I concur. We know it as *The Parable of the Prodigal Son.* It is no doubt the favorite of many, many congregations and also the favorite subject of many and many a preacher. In the story you can almost hear the flapping of his rags as the Prodigal returns, and you might even hear the crunching of the swine's pods when he is in the far country. But this great, great story deals with some very important subjects for our lives. I have titled it, "Give Me, Give Me, Give Me," and I think as we progress, you will see why, if you haven't already grasped it. It is a play in at least three acts. The *dramatis personae* consist of the Prodigal Son, the loving father, and the older brother.

It begins, "A certain man had two sons" (Luke 15:11). Poor man, he really got quite a pair—a rake and a churl. I don't know which was worse, but he had both in his house, and he was a loving and gracious man. From the very beginning we see that this younger son had dreamed a dream. Now there is nothing wrong with dreams. In fact, many of the greatest things in this world began with dreams. Columbus dreamed a dream, and a whole continent, or even two, sprang from the waters. Edison dreamed a dream and night disappeared!

There are, of course, bad dreams as well—nightmares we call them, but our young Prodigal dreamed his own dream. It was a dream about the "far country." Now where is that precisely? Was that referring to Rome, or perhaps to Corinth—a wild town. Or maybe it wasn't so far away in terms of miles at all. It was the content of the dream, not the distance that mattered. He dreamed a dream of the far country—a country where he would be free from the galling supervision of his father, and most particularly the criticism of his churlish elder brother; you just couldn't do enough right to satisfy him. He was going to get away from all of this, and he never wanted to see or hear about it again!

"GIVE ME THE PORTION"

So he came to his father and said, "Father, give me the portion of goods that falls to me" (Luke 15:12). Now here is a philosophy of economics that I think is not altogether uncommon today—"Give me." This is the view of economics that many people have—no doubt some right here in this room! That is why I titled the message today, "Give me, Give Me, Give Me." All over the country people are looking for someone to give them something for free.

Give me! "Give me that portion of the goods that falls to me." Some people seem to have the idea that money comes on trees. Sometimes you have to pick it off like leaves; other times it just falls on you. Well, that seems to be this young man's idea. As we read further, we see all kinds of philosophical, theological, and economic views—"'Give me the portion of the goods that falls to me' . . . which I deserve! You see, I get all of this money that my father now has, but which, unfortunately, he is going to give part of to that churlish brother of mine. But there is a portion of it that's mine, and I want it—and I want it now. So give me, give me, give me!" Well, that's just not the way the world works in most cases. Money doesn't fall off of trees. Furthermore, he didn't really know it, but it wasn't necessarily his at all.

However, this young man was quite sure that he had at least half of a huge estate that was coming to him, and he wanted it now! He didn't want to wait until he was too old to enjoy it. He wanted it right now. So, his father—without argument, without objection—"divided to them his livelihood" (Luke 15:12). Now there was a *very* generous father, indeed. Not many days later the young man gathered all of his things together and took his journey into a "far country."

"A FAR COUNTRY"

This "far country" means anywhere that Daddy and brother are not. It could be just a few miles away, or it could be across the world. But wherever it was, he was going to have fun in the far country. Christ expresses it with a great economy of words, "There [he] wasted his substance with riotous living" (Luke 15:13 KJV). Does anyone need that explained? We can all think of examples—we see them all around; you are living right in the middle of much of America's "far country." They come down here by the hundreds of thousands to get away—to get away from marriages that are unhappy, to get away from parents, to get away from all kinds of things, and to have a great time. So he "wasted his substance with riotous living."

Then this amazing concurrence of events and divine providence took place; "But when he had spent all, there arose a severe famine in that land, and he began to be in want" (Luke 15:14). Remember the Old Testament story of General Sisera? He fought against the Israelites, and we read that "the stars in their courses fought against Sisera." I don't know how literally you are going to take that battle. I don't think the stars drew swords and began to throw them at him, but we understand basically what is meant. So we see that this mighty famine came into the land. When? Not when he first arrived, when his pocketbook was full, but after he had wasted all of his substance.

We see the concurrence between our activities and our sin, and God's providence in the land. How many people have conjectured about why we have had this hurricane or that hurricane, or this flood, or whatever it might be? I don't pretend to be some infallible interpreter of divine providence, but I think it doesn't take too much to ascertain some pretty obvious reasons why this mighty famine had arisen in the land.

"AND HE BEGAN TO BE IN WANT"

Now, he had never ever been in want. He lived in a home where all of his needs were regularly provided by his obviously well-to-do father, who had worked long and hard and had built up the family fortune and supplied his every need. He is suddenly going from a wild, wealthy young man—"Hail fellow well-met, organizer of parties, buyers of drinks," and "It's all on me, fellas; step up to the bar"—to a man with nothing!

Furthermore, he has come to that position in a far country—far from his father, far from the farm, far from anything, and it's a bad time to be there, because famine stalks the land. So we are told that he joined himself to a citizen of that country. This was no doubt a wonderful person, because he had gotten away from all of the mean, nasty people at home, going to the far country, where everyone was wonderful. So what did this wonderful man do? "He sent him into his fields to feed swine" (Luke 15:15). Now our young Prodigal must have thought, "What in the world is a fine young Jewish boy like me doing out here feeding pigs?" But feed the pigs he did, and he envied the pigs. "He would gladly have filled his stomach with the pods that the swine ate."

Another little picture in our photogravure of the far country says, "And no one gave him anything" (Luke 15:16). You see—he was a *taker*. What he discovered in the far country was that everybody else was, too! Oh, they were so happy to meet him—"Hail fellow, well met, giver of big parties, buyer of drinks." However, now the famine was in the land, and no one gave him anything, because you see, not only was *he* a taker, so was *everyone else* in the far country.

How many times people have come to this church when it was clear to see (if you believed in such a thing) that they were "down on their luck." Where do they come? They come to the church and ask for "money for food." So we would give them a ticket that was good for food—and only food—at a nearby restaurant. Some people practically threw these tickets back in our faces! There were times when I was sorely tempted to say to them, "I know you *really* want something to drink, and there's a bar just a few blocks down the street. I'm sure that if you go there and tell the barkeeper that you've spent all your money—and even some of it in his place—he would be happy to give you some money in your time of need." No. He wouldn't! Where do people go to get help in times of need? They don't go to a bar—they go to the *church*. That is what this young man did when "he came to himself."

"HE CAME TO HIMSELF"

"No one gave him *anything*" (Luke 15:16), so he was in bad,

bad shape. At this point we read that "he came to himself" (Luke 15:17). An interesting phrase—"he came to himself." The Bible makes it very clear that sin is not this sophisticated, intelligent kind of life that the media would make you think. Scripture says that sin is folly—that it is foolishness. "The fool has said in his heart, 'There is no God' . . . They have done abominable works" (Psalm 14:1). If you've ever thought, "Well, atheists are good moral people too"—that is not what the Bible says. Note again: "The fool has said in his heart, '*There is* no God,' . . . They have done abominable works." Atheism is the greatest excuse for abominations that man has ever dreamed of!

"He came to himself"—it is as if he were out of his mind! Perhaps he was in some kind of psychotic condition—he was *not himself*. There had been something wrong with him, but now "he came to himself." Actually, that's literally what happens when a person comes to God—they are brought into their *right mind*. They are quickened and made intelligent again, able to think logically.

We next read that "when he came to himself, he said . . . ." Now he is having a discussion with himself, which is a good thing. The Scriptures in a number of places urge us to have a talk with ourselves. "He came to himself," and he said, "How many of my father's hired servants have bread enough and to spare, and I perish with hunger!" (Luke 15:17). He once had a bag full of money, and now his bag was empty. If your own wallet or purse were empty, you might have a very enlightening conversation with yourself too. An empty pocketbook has given some real wisdom to many a would-be prodigal over the years. As he looks into his empty bag and feels his equally empty stomach, and as his face is pinched with hunger, he is getting some very realistic answers.

So he says, "I will arise and go to my father, and will say to him, 'Father, I have sinned against heaven and before you'" (Luke 15:18). Now that's the essence of *repentance*—yet how many people I have heard say something like that, and a few weeks later they were right back where they were before. Notice what Christ says here about repentance. The young man said, "I will arise and go to my father, and will say to him, 'Father, I have sinned.'"And what did he do? He arose and he went and he said, "I have sinned." He did exactly what he said he would do. He had come to his right mind and was not going to be deluded by lies and fairy tales any more. He had seen the far country for what it really is—ugly. It is very ugly—in spite of all the attempts of the media to paint it as glamorous, glorious, wondrous, and fun. He started out with a dream, and he ended up with a nightmare. That's the far country!

"MAKE ME"

In the second act of this great drama, we see a very patient and loving father. The Prodigal had been preparing his speech to his father: "I am no longer worthy to be called your son. Make me like one of your hired servants" (Luke 15:19). Notice the enormous reversal in what he had originally said to his father— this is indicative of what a true Christian experience is. His very first words had been, "Give me!" "Give me the portion of goods that falls to me." "Give me, give me, give me!" But now he is going to say to his father something quite antithetical to that— he is not saying "*give* me," but "*make* me." "Make me like one of your hired servants!" (Luke 15:19). He says, "I am no longer worthy to be called your son. Make me like one of your hired servants" (Luke 15:19).

He used to be a son—eligible to receive half of the fortune at his whim. Now, he can't ask for anything. There is not one single syllable of "give me" in his speech. Instead it is, "Father, I am no longer worthy to be called your son. Make me like one of your servants." He didn't ask for a big meal. He was hoping he might get sent back by an angry father—back to the kitchen! "Get back there and get to work, and maybe they will give you something to eat before you go to sleep." That was all he was expecting. He had gone from "gimme" to "make me."

What are your prayers? Which of these phrases dominates? How many Christians would have to admit that the vast majority of their prayers are, "Father, give me this, and give me that, and give me the other thing"? "Give me this favor, give me that favor." But thank God for those that say, "Father, *make me* truly your servant. *Make me* a good servant. *Make me* a follower of Jesus

Christ. *Make me* a witness for your grace. *Make me* what *you* would have me to be." What a difference between the philosophy of life of the "gimme" person and the "make me" person! Which would you say that you are? Which predominates? I would be surprised if, for most people, the majority of their prayers aren't "give me!" However, God wants people who want Him and want to be His servants and want to follow Him.

"HIS FATHER RAN!"

The father was apparently sitting on the roof of his house—the common place to sit in those days—where you got a little bit more of a breeze. Up there was no doubt a table and places for shade—umbrellas, where you could sit and have a meal, talk, read, and pray. I am sure this father did a lot of praying, and he asked God for his son—not *give me*, but "Lord, *give him* a heart that longs for you and his father's house!"

This father is a great example. He had two sons, a rake and a churl—not a very happy family, indeed. Nevertheless, he loved them—not because of what they had done, but he loved them in spite of everything they had done—not because of what they were, but in spite of what they were. That's grace, and that's our only hope with God! The father, of course, in this parable is a picture of the Father in Heaven.

Significantly, in reading the Old Testament, we never read that God ran. He *walked* with Adam in the Garden. He *walked* here. He *walked* there. He *walked* through this. We read numerous times that God walked, but we never read that He *ran*—except here, when this father of the Prodigal saw his long-lost son one day, after weeks, months or even years. It never says how long the Prodigal had been gone—but the father was waiting faithfully and lovingly, as a father who loved his sons. When he saw his son approaching, he dropped everything and rapidly made his way down the stairs on the side of the house, and to the astonishment of his servants, he *ran* down the path! He had first seen the silhouette of a head—the hair was longer, but it looked familiar—then the entire torso appeared as someone was coming up the path a great way off. He said, "It is my *son*! My *son* is *home*!" And he *ran* as fast as he could—with his robes flapping in the breeze. His hands are outstretched . . . and the Prodigal is reviewing his speech one more time . . . .

Just as he gets to the father, who *flings* his arms around his neck and begins to hug him and kiss him on the cheek and the forehead over and over again, the boy tries to say, "I have sinned against heaven and in your sight, and am no longer worthy...." But the father was kissing him again and again. Finally, as he tries to finish his speech, the father speaks and says to the servants, "Bring out the best robe...." It says the *first* robe in Greek, which was a special robe for the special son, and now *he* is that son! The father gives further instructions. "Put a ring on his hand and sandals on *his* feet" (Luke 15:22). The father puts the family ring on his finger and has the special calf that had been saved for occasions like this killed and served. "Let there be dancing and music and feasting, for this my son was dead and is alive!"

"NOW HIS OLDER SON DREW NEAR"

What a wonderful place to end the story—yet it doesn't end there. Here is the last act of this great drama—and the background music changes to a minor key. We read in the text that the older son was in the field, and he approached the house at night, after a whole day of work. He heard the music and the rejoicing and the dancing in the home and called to one of the servants and said to him, "What is this sound? This music?" The servant—ignorant of the true nature of the heart of this young man—says to him, "Your brother has come, and because he has received him safe and sound, your father has killed the fatted calf" (Luke 15:27).

Then the older brother rejoiced also, and he and the servant danced a circle out on the lawn. Well . . . no. What we read is, "But he was angry and would not go in. Therefore, his father came out and pleaded with him. So he answered and said to *his* father, 'Lo, these many years I have been serving you; I never transgressed your commandment at any time; and yet you never gave me a young goat that I might make merry with my friends. But as soon as this son of yours came, who has devoured your livelihood with harlots, you killed the fatted calf for him'" (Luke 15:28-30). "No," he says, "I will not go in."

Notice that the older son never calls him "my brother." It's always "This son of yours," but the father always says, "Your brother." The older son complained, "But as soon as *this son of yours* came, who has devoured your livelihood with harlots, you killed the fatted calf for him" (Luke 15:30). Question—how did he know that his brother had devoured the living with harlots? He hadn't seen or heard from him in years. How did he know that? Certainly the servant didn't know. How did the older brother know? I suspect that he was more familiar with the far country than he let on, because you don't have to go 150 miles away—you can find the "far country" right close to home. It can be a dream in your mind when you are safe at home—supposedly keeping your father's business going.

This reminds us there are two kinds of sinners. There are those who are guilty of *license*, as the Prodigal Son was, by throwing off all laws and going out and living riotously. Then there is the *legalist*. The legalist will outwardly keep the letter of the law and be very punctilious about that, and yet, in his heart he may be living in the far country. But *both* license and legalism are grievous sins. In this parable, Christ was talking to both such people, and He was identifying with them both. The question is, which group are you in? I am sure that somewhere in this magnificent parable there is a place for you. This is an inclusive parable and you and I are both in it somewhere. Which is your proclivity—*license* or *legalism*?

The father said to the older son, "Son, you are always with me, and all that I have is yours. It was right that we should make merry and be glad, for your brother was dead and is alive again, and was lost and is found" (Luke 15:31-32). This is a picture of salvation—going from death to life (Luke 15:24). Paul tells us, "And you He made alive, who were dead in trespasses and sins" (Ephesians 2:1).

That is what Christ has done for us; He made us alive out of the deadness of sin. So, I would ask you this question—do you *know* that you have passed from death unto life? That's what is meant by the phrase—"born again." Many church members today don't have a clue what that is. They cannot say that Christ has changed their lives and brought them out of deadness into life. I hope you can, because Jesus Christ, the King of the kingdom said, "I say to you, unless one is born again, he cannot see the kingdom of God" (John 3:3).

Dear friend, where are you in this parable? I hope you will find out now, while there is still a chance to begin all over again, and come to Christ. What a difference it would have made if the older brother had done that! He would have come into the house. He would have clasped his younger rogue brother in his arms and told him how good it was to have him back again— told him how much he had missed him, and he would have rejoiced at his return home! That would truly be a picture of heaven—and that is what Christ would like the picture of *every church* and *every heart* to be!

CHAPTER SIX

A MATTER OF PROFIT AND LOSS*

In this final chapter, we look at two "enterprises," the earthly and the heavenly. The ultimate hope for all Christians is that our treasures are not here on earth, where moths and rust can destroy and thieves can steal. Our true treasures are in heaven— and that knowledge can give us perspective on what is happening in our present-day economy, as we remember our Lord's words, "For where your treasure is, there your heart will be also." —Matthew 6:21

* This was originally preached by Dr. D. James Kennedy at Coral Ridge Presbyterian Church in Fort Lauderdale, Florida, on November 18, 1984.

> *"For what will it profit a man if he gains
> the whole world, and loses his own soul?"*
> —Mark 8:36

Charlemagne, Charles the Magnificent, was no doubt the greatest monarch of the Middle Ages. He ruled over virtually all of Europe. His wealth was infinite, his power almost without limit. As death approached, his distinct faith in Jesus Christ as his Savior caused him to plan a most unusual funeral for himself, and, thus, he was buried at the magnificent Aix-la-Chapelle under the huge dome, dressed in his royal robes and seated on a magnificent throne gilded with gold and precious jewels. The royal crown rested on his head, and on his lap lay an open Bible, the forefinger of his right hand pointing at the words: "For what shall it profit a man if he shall gain the whole world and lose his own soul?"

Though long dead, Charlemagne may yet speak to the culture of America today, for the lesson he was trying to teach is one that most Americans have not yet learned—namely, that there are no pockets in a shroud. We can take none of this world's goods with us as we leave. A wealthy man died some time ago, and someone was heard to inquire, "How much did he leave?" The response was, "All of it!" Yet it would seem that most people in this land, in fact in most of the lands of this globe, have been deluded by the Great Deceiver into believing that our purpose in this life is to amass as large a chunk of the world's goods as we possibly can.

FIRST THINGS FIRST

Please imagine the following scenario: The President of the United States has a six-year-old son who comes to his father and says, "Daddy, I would like to set up a lemonade stand in front of the White House."

His father encourages him, saying "All right, son, go right ahead."

Late that afternoon the little boy comes in all wide-eyed and excited saying, "Daddy, Daddy, guess what? I made a dollar and twenty-three cents today!"

"Oh," responds the President, with unusual interest, "That's wonderful, son."

The next day his father goes out to observe and is struck by the fact that, indeed, business is brisk. The fact of the matter is that the boy made twice as much on the second day. The third day the father offers to help, and so the President of the United States could be found out on the street cutting lemons in half and squeezing them to make the lemonade.

The fifth day his wife speaks to him with some concern and says, "Honey, do you really think you should be spending your time making lemonade? Aren't there other things you should be doing?"

He responds, "But, dear, you don't understand, we made $4.80 today. The way business is growing, why, there is no telling what this might develop into!"

The second week he is out there from morning until night. His Chief of Staff, of course, is ready to pull out his hair. Other aides are quite concerned, and they say to him, "Mr. President, do you realize that there are four ambassadors waiting to see you, two treaties that need to be signed, and the budget must be presented to Congress? Don't you understand?"

The President replies, "But don't you see? We made $12.40 yesterday. Business is growing at a phenomenal rate. Why, at the end of the year, I compute that we should have made $32,214!"

What would you think if you read such a story in the *Wall Street Journal*? You wouldn't suppose that your President needed to be voted out of office, but rather that he needed to be placed in an institution for the mentally incompetent! Yet, dear friends, in all kindness, there are some of you who are more foolish than he.

TWO TYPES OF ENTERPRISES

Each of us is engaged in two types of enterprises. On the one hand there are enterprises we undertake with our bodies—our flesh and bone and our senses. For most people, these take up most, if not all, of their time, energy, thoughts, and concern. Yet we are engaged in another enterprise of far greater import—an enterprise that is, by its very nature, eternal and infinite in scope. I refer to the enterprise of our soul.

The President of the United States was not elected by the people to run a lemonade stand. You were not created by an eternal God to wallow in the mud flats of materialism. God has called us to far greater and higher things. "For what will it profit a man if he gains the whole world, and loses his own soul?" (Mark 8:36).

Jim Elliott, the famous missionary to the Auca Indians, put it so well in his diary: "He is no fool who gives up that which he cannot keep in order to gain that which he cannot lose." The reverse of that is the very height of folly! What will a man give in exchange for his soul?

If you look around today, you would suppose that our souls are of very little value. Looking at television, you might be convinced that man has no soul at all, or that its concerns are far beneath the attention of any intelligent man. When did you last see anyone on television demonstrate any concern for his eternal soul? We are bombarded by propaganda on all sides that says that our souls are of no value at all, and the things of this world are of surpassing importance. Therefore, we should give our complete attention to them. All of these things would conspire to say that Jesus was wrong when He supremely, imperiously surveys the whole of humanity and all human endeavors and says to us, "For what will it profit a man if he gains the whole world, and loses his own soul?"

Many of you may be businessmen or women accustomed to examining profit and loss columns—accustomed to examining the bottom line. About that you are very astute and very clever. Yet, my friends, many of you have left out of your reckoning altogether the matter of the eternal welfare of your soul.

WHAT IS YOUR SOUL WORTH?

One little girl asked her father, "Daddy, is your soul insured?"

Puzzled, he responded, "No, darling, why do you ask?"

"Well, you were just saying that your car is insured, and our house is insured, and last week I heard Uncle George say that he was afraid you would lose your soul. Daddy, is your soul insured?"

Dear friend, I would ask that question of you today. Is your soul insured? Your life is insured, your house is insured, your car is insured, but many of you are walking around "soul naked" with not one bit of insurance for your soul.

After a careful evaluation, some people might think it a fair bargain, and in order to gain the whole world, they might even be willing to give up their souls. However, they would be fools, to say the least! The real tragedy is that most people are willing to sell their souls for hardly a smidgen of the world. In fact, it is astonishing how cheaply some people are willing to sell their souls. How much is yours worth?

What Jesus Christ is saying here is that your soul is worth more than all the wealth of this world piled up in one place! All of its gold and silver and precious jewels heaped into one great mountain are nothing, by comparison, to the value of your soul. You are an *eternal being* created in the image of the everlasting God, and you shall live forever. When the vast myriad of stars that make up the Milky Way have burned themselves out in a black disk, your soul will only then just have begun to live and shall never ever, ever, ever, ever die! What shall a man give in exchange for his soul?

A DAY OF RECKONING OR REWARD?

When he comes to the moment of his death, what shall it profit a man to have gained the whole world? Many have learned only too late how foolish a bargain they have made in this world. Cesare Borgia, son of Pope Alexander VI, was a great prince and is immortalized as the personification of a prince in Machiavelli's *The Prince*. He was devious and consummately dexterous in dealing with men and affairs. He was prepared for every extremity, for every circumstance of life. However, in his memoirs, written shortly before his death in 1507, he said, "I have provided in the course of my life for everything except death. Now, alas, I am to die entirely unprepared."

Edward Gibbon, who wrote *The Decline and Fall of the Roman Empire*, was a great skeptic. He came to Paris from England as a young man and fell in with the fashionable infidelity of that time. Subsequently, he wrote many things attacking Christ and Christianity. Then he, too, as all men must, came to that great appointment with the enemy—death. In London, England, in 1794 he said, "All is now lost, irrecoverably lost. All is dark and doubtful," and then he died.

When the great French statesman Talleyrand came at last to his deathbed, King Louis asked him how he felt. Talleyrand replied, "Sire, I am suffering the pangs of the damned."

In 1821, Sir Thomas Scott reached the end of his long and illustrious career as Privy Counselor to King James the Sixth of Scotland. On his deathbed he uttered these unforgettable words, "Until this moment I believed that there was neither a God nor a hell, but now I know that there are both, and I am doomed to perdition by the just sentence of the Almighty," and he expired.

And what of Clarence Darrow? A brilliant, witty, sarcastic, and articulate lawyer, he earned fame in the great Scopes Monkey Trial of 1925, and accordingly, he is held up before the eyes of so many skeptical lawyers today. His physician records that when he came to his last illness, he called for three clergymen. (Being a careful lawyer, he was not going to be satisfied with one.) When the ministers arrived, he said, "Gentlemen, during my lifetime I have written and spoken many things against God and the churches, and now I could wish that I had not, for I realize that it is entirely possible that I was wrong. So I would like to ask you one last favor—that each of you would intercede for me with the Almighty." Where was that biting irony now? Where was his bitter skepticism when it came to that last day?

An atheist physician propagandized his views to others, giving many of them books. One young man who had received them renounced his belief in Christ and God and became, himself, an unbeliever. Some years later, the young man came to his final illness, and the unbelieving physician attended him. The physician said, "Young man, I want you to die as you have lived—a rejecter of Christ and of God," and as the young man lay suffering, the physician said, "Hold on!"

"But, Doctor," the young man replied. "That is just my trouble. You gave me *nothing* to hold on to." The doctor had no reply.

How different are those experiences from the death experiences of believers. Phillip Jenks, a humble Christian, came to his final illness, and a friend said to him, "How hard is it to die, Phillip?"

Jenks responded, "I have experienced more happiness in two hours today, when dying, than in my life. I have long desired that I might glorify God in my death, but I never thought that such a poor worm as I could come to such a glorious death." How vastly different is the death of a believer!

THE DAY OF JUDGMENT

What shall it profit a man when he comes to his deathbed to have gained the whole world? What shall it profit him when he shall come to the final judgment bar of God, to the *Great Assize*, when all mankind shall be summoned before that final bar of justice? We shall be stripped of all our earthly possessions, and we shall stand naked before the judgment of Him whose eyes are too pure to look upon iniquity. We shall give an account of our lives before the whole world. What shall it matter what material possessions have been ours? What shall it profit a man to have gained the whole world when he comes to that judgment and hears the final awesome terrible verdict, "Depart from Me, you cursed, into the everlasting fire prepared for the devil and his angels" (Matthew 25:41). What shall it profit him when he sinks down into hell forever and ever?

Ah, but today the modern, fashionable skepticism of our age says that there is no such thing as hell. If there is a hell, then most surely we experience it in this world! Like the previous testimonies, many countless thousands have come to realize that that, too, is a lie.

DEATH IS NOT PEACE

There was a church member who was neither an atheist

nor a skeptic. He was a professed believer in Christ, at least nominally so, but inwardly his heart was untouched. Many in our churches today have professed faith with their lips, but they do not possess it in their hearts. Their hearts are far from God. They have never truly repented of their sins. They have never surrendered their lives to Jesus Christ.

One day this church member suddenly and unexpectedly closed his eyes in death and found himself floating rapidly downward through a tunnel lined with fire. Many have related a similar floating sensation that led them to a bright light, but his experience was very different. He came to a dark, black cavern and saw friends from the "good ole' days." They were loaded down with huge, heavy burdens and were moving around continually, but going nowhere. They dared not stop because of the fear of the "main drivers," which were beings, he said, that were beyond description. Total darkness surrounded those engaged in this pointless activity. This man was suddenly summoned away by the power of God and returned to tell that story.

Then there was a young lady who attempted to commit suicide by taking a whole bottle of aspirin. As the doctor was striving to restore her life, her eyes suddenly flickered open and she began to cry, "Momma, Momma, help me. Make them let me go. They are trying to hurt me, Momma." The doctor step-ped back apologetically, thinking she was referring to him. She said, "No. Not the doctor. It's them, it's them, those demons in hell; they wouldn't let go of me. They wanted me. I couldn't get back. Oh, Momma, it was just terrible. It was just awful." Would that every young person in our schools today could hear that testimony! "For what will it profit a man if he gains the whole world, and loses his own soul?"

Countless young people in our country today are following her example. Our culture, saturated in secularism, says that there is nothing beyond the grave. If you have trouble in this life, escape is simple—end your life and you will be at peace. That is the Devil's lie!

CHRIST PAID IT ALL

How can you lose your soul? You can lose it by denying

Christ—by rejecting Him. Or you can lose it by simply neglecting Him. "How shall we escape," says the Scripture, "if we neglect so great a salvation" (Hebrews 2:3). I believe that more people perish this way than by outright denial—by simple neglect, by merely putting it off, by being satisfied with the external, the mere shell of religion. They have only a nominal profession and have not truly surrendered their lives to Christ. That is how we can lose our souls.

Christ said, "If anyone desires to come after me, let him . . . take up his cross, and follow Me" (Matthew 16:24). We must be willing to give up our lives if we are to find them. We must receive Him as Savior and Lord of our lives. That is how we can save our souls—only by looking to Him, that One on the middle Cross, who was lifted up between heaven and hell, there to endure in His own body and soul the infinite agonies of Hell—to take upon Himself our guilt, our transgressions, our iniquity. He suffered in our stead the bitter penalty of sin, until at last He could cry out, "It is finished." It is done. It is paid.

Now, having risen from the dead and ascended into heaven, He freely offers us a gift. Let me say that again—He *freely* offers to us the gift of *everlasting* life. How tragic, how doubly tragic it is that any should perish and lose their souls, when life everlasting is offered so freely. If we were told that we must climb Mount Everest to obtain the eternal salvation of our soul, millions would attempt it—but many would not be able. My friend, we are told that this gift is absolutely *free*—that it was paid for by another at infinite cost. Yet it may be ours if we will place our trust in Christ—if we will place our hope in Him—if we will invite Him into our lives—if we will surrender ourselves in repentance to Him as our Savior and Lord.

THE TWO OPTIONS

Have you done that, dear friend? If you have not, then you have made a bargain with the Devil, and you are a consummate fool! Knowingly or unknowingly, decidedly or simply by neglect, that failure to act upon the promise of Christ will cost you your eternal soul.

Some of the decisions confronting us in life present two very different options—two very separate choices. However, while we are in the process of deciding, we are already following one of these options. Let me illustrate: If your car has stalled on the railroad track and you see the train approaching, you have two options. You may either stay in the car and try to start it in order to save both yourself and your automobile—or you may leap out of the car and run for your life. You may not save your car, but at least you will save your skin!

There are two options before you right now. While you are considering them, you are already following one of them. You are in the car, and the train is coming. The two options before you are: Will you surrender your heart to Jesus Christ and give yourself over to God, or will you continue to ignore Him, continue to neglect Him, and continue to live for the things of this world? As you contemplate those two options, do not forget that you are living out one of them. If you have not yet received the Savior, you are still lost. You are still under the condemnation of God. The juggernaut of God's judgment is bearing down upon your soul. "For what will it profit a man if he gains the whole world, and loses his own soul?"

My prayer is that the almighty and everlasting God, who has created us in His own image, will bring each of us to a conviction of the truth of our own immortality—that He will impress on us the truth that we shall live *forever*, either in the bliss and felicity of heaven or in the pain and well-deserved punishment of hell. Dear friend, if in your heart you realize that you have neglected the well-being of your eternal soul, I urge you to pray: "O, Christ, come into my life. I have foolishly ignored You. I have lived for the things of this world that are passing away, but I know that some day my life here will end. I want to live with you forever in heaven. I invite You to come into my heart, to forgive me, to cleanse me and to renew me. Clothe me in the white robes of Jesus Christ's righteousness. I accept Him as my Savior and Lord and Master of my life. In His name, I pray, Amen."

If you have prayed this prayer asking Jesus Christ to be your Savior and Lord, we would like to help and encourage you in your new life in Christ by sending you a copy of Dr. Kennedy's book, Beginning Again. *To request a copy, please write to Coral Ridge Ministries, P.O. Box 1920, Fort Lauderdale, FL 33302, or contact us at 1-800-988-7884.*